MAKE YOUR MOVE

26 Best 1 v 1 Soccer Moves

Alfred Galustian and Charlie Cooke

THE LYONS PRESS
Guilford, Connecticut
An imprint of The Globe Pequot Press

LAD 1/09
Use 4

Adapted from *Make Your Move* (original material designed and edited by Coachwise Business Solutions, Leeds, UK, 2004). Coachwise Business Solutions provides a range of design and editorial services. For more information about these, please contact Head of Publications or Head of Design in the UK at 0113-231-1310 or email publications@coachwise.ltd.uk.

The Lyons Press is an imprint of The Globe Pequot Press.

The word Coerver® and the Coerver® Coaching logo are registered trademarks of Sportsmethod Ltd and Sportsmethod Asia Ltd.

10 9 8 7 6 5 4 3 2 1

Printed in China

ISBN 1-59228-698-4

Library of Congress Cataloging-in-Publication Data is available on file.

Authors
Alfred Galustian, Charlie cooke

Editors
Lucy Hyde, Joe Provey

Designers
Sandra Flintham, saima Nazir, Leanne Taylor

Illustrations
John Kanzler

Photographs
Carlos Furtado, EMPICS

The authors would like to thank:

Paul Bentvelzen (Coerver® Coaching Oceania), Brad Douglass (Coerver® Coaching Sweden) and Seiji Nakayama (Coerver® Coaching Japan), and the Coerver® Coaching kids from Sweden, USA and Oceania who took part in this project.

This book is dedicated to our teacher, Wiel Coerver, and to Gérard Houllier, who represent the very best in soccer education.

Published with
Coerver Coaching USA
3912 Eastern Avenue
Cincinnatti, OH 45226
Tel: 513-321-5078 Fax: 513-321-6552
www.coerver-coaching.com

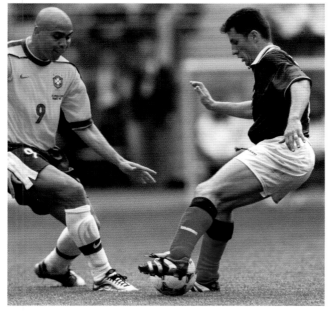

*John Collins (Scotland), former Coerver pupil, plays 1 v 1
versus Ronaldo (Brazil)*

Contents

Foreword

It's a pleasure for me to write this foreword for my good friends Alfred Galustian and Charlie Cooke, whose work I admire greatly.

Alfred and Charlie have dedicated their coaching careers to devising skill-training programmes for youth coaches and players around the world.

Teaching skills should, in my opinion, be the foundation of all soccer coaching, especially at the young formative years. I feel the Coerver® Coaching Programme is the ideal way to do this.

I first studied the Coerver® Coaching Programme at The Coerver® Coaching Academy in Japan and since then, have been convinced it's the key value for both players and coaches.

I especially like their work in 1 v 1 training. Any player who has good 1 v 1 skills can often make a difference in a game, creating goal chances for himself or his teammates.

I wish the Coerver® Coaching Programme had been available when I was a player!

Jürgen Klinsmann
German World Cup Champion

Alfred Galustian

Alfred Galustian is the co-founder and International Director of Coerver® Coaching. He is responsible for establishing programmes in Asia, Africa, Australia, Europe and the Americas.

Alfred started his soccer career as a player with Wimbledon, after which he obtained his coaching licences in England and the USA.

He has worked as a technical coaching instructor at the French, Brazilian, Japanese and Chinese Football Federations and with top professional clubs including Bayern Munich (Germany), AC Milan (Italy), Auxerre and Olympique Marseille (France), Real Madrid (Spain) and Newcastle United and Arsenal (England).

He has received written commendations from FIFA for his contribution to soccer development around the world.

Alfred is also the International Technical Consultant for Special Olympics (Soccer).

Charlie Cooke

Charlie Cooke is the co-founder of Coerver® Coaching and Director of North, Central and South America, where he directs hundreds of Coerver® Coaching soccer camps.

As a player, Charlie starred for Aberdeen FC and Dundee FC in Scotland's First Division before joining Chelsea FC in the English First Division. At Chelsea he won the English Football Association Cup and the European Cup Winners Cup. He represented Scotland in international matches 16 times and was selected for the World All Star Team in 1967.

Charlie completed his career as a player with the Los Angeles Aztecs of the North American Soccer League before accepting head coaching posts with both the Memphis Rogues of the NASL and the Wichita Wings of the Major Indoor Soccer League.

Together with Alfred, Charlie has authored several books and videos on Coerver® Coaching and skill development methods.

Introduction

When broken down moment by moment, the game of soccer is largely a series of 1 v 1 *Moves*. In a single professional match you can expect to find over 200 such occurrences. While the use of moves is not suitable for all 1 v 1 competitions, many opportunities are missed because players don't utilise this important skill. As such, we believe 1 v 1 moves should be a crucial part of every player's repertoire.

Teaching moves, however, is not a simple matter. As well as mastering *How* to execute a move, players must learn which move to make and *When* and *Where* to make it. In this book, we hope to provide key guidance on making these decisions for coaches, teachers and players.

The 1 v 1 Moves Pyramid© shows our three basic categories of moves: *Changes of Direction*, *Stops and Starts*, and *Feints*.

Changes of direction are used to shield the ball and to turn into space.

Stops and starts create space by using changes of pace.

Feints create space to either side of an opponent so that you can shoot, pass or run with the ball.

This book features eight of Coerver's favourite basic moves. Each basic move has several variations. For example, one of the feints featured is the classic Step-over Move. It has three variations; the Double Step-over, the Pull Through Step-over and the Slap Step-over. Together, these four moves comprise one *move set*, Move Set F on page 49.

Knowing how to make all the moves is only half the battle for a player, coach or teacher. Unfortunately, it's impossible to categorically say exactly when and where players should use each 1 v 1 skill. Each situation on the field is different. In any case, the coach can have very little influence during play. It is the player who must decide which move to use, often in a split second. In this book, however, we will suggest when and where 1 v 1 moves can work, and enable the coach to help prepare players to make the right decisions.

The Importance of 1 v 1 Moves

1 v 1 skills are useful for every outfield player, regardless of their position. Coerver® Coaching is 1 v 1 teaching at its best.

Osvaldo Ardiles
Argentina World Cup Champion

Over ten years ago, while Technical Director of the French Federation, I invited Alfred Galustian to work with our national and regional coaches at our National Training Centre ... I asked him to focus on skills, especially 1 v 1, as taught in the Coerver® Coaching Programme. The influence of Coerver® Coaching in France has continued to this day and, in my opinion, has been a big factor in producing many of our new rising stars.

Gérard Houllier
Manager, Liverpool FC
Technical Director of France
World Cup Champions, 1998

While 1 v 1 is only one part of the Coerver® Coaching curriculum, it is an important topic to us for several reasons:

1   Players with good 1 v 1 skills can often make the difference in a game, creating goal chances even though outnumbered by opponents.

2   1 v 1 drills and games are great ways of improving speed, stamina and strength.

3   Players with good 1 v 1 skills usually develop an inner-confidence. Confidence can be the vital factor in players reaching the highest levels of the game.

After many years of experience in teaching this area, we believe young players are best taught such skills between the ages of seven and 15. At these ages, the coordination and fluency needed for good 1 v 1 skills are developed relatively quickly. Once these skills have been learned, many players are able to use them more spontaneously in full pressure game situations.

How to Use This Book

Each section allows the coach to focus on one set of moves at a time. Each move and move variation is detailed with step-by-step photos to assist the coach in correctly demonstrating it. These are accompanied by important tips, including where and when the moves are effective.

A skill drill follows each set of moves. This is designed for use during training sessions and will improve players' technique through repetition. All eight skill drills are used with little or no pressure so that players can learn the skills well through unbroken repetition.

We also include ten skill games. These are full pressure activities. They enable the coach and player to see if the learned skills can be used effectively under full game pressure from opponents.

Most of the moves can be practised in any of the skill drills or skill games, and players should try to practise all the moves with both right and left foot.

This book is not only useful for helping coaches and teachers introduce the skills and games in their practice sessions. It can also be used by the players; to learn the skills for themselves.

Please note: Throughout this book, the pronouns he, she, him, her and so on are interchangeable, and intended to be inclusive of both male and female. It is important in sport, as elsewhere, that both genders have equal status and opportunities.

The History of Coerver® Coaching

Wiel Coerver with soccer legend Sir Stanley Matthews

Coerver® Coaching had its start in the late 1970s when Dutch European Championship winning coach Wiel Coerver led a revolution in soccer coaching. He was dissatisfied with the lack of individual skills and emphasis on defensive play in the professional game, which were stifling the more exciting, attacking style of play necessary to score goals and attract fans.

Up to that point, little attention had been given to individual skill development, because no one knew quite how to teach these skills. It was also widely assumed that the great players of the game were innately gifted, far beyond the capabilities of the average player.

Coerver's early focus was on teaching ball mastery and 1 v 1 skills by encouraging players to emulate the moves of soccer's all-time greats such as Sir Stanley Matthews, Cryuff, Beckenbauer and Pele.

In 1983, Wiel Coerver was joined by Alfred Galustian and Charlie Cooke. Together, they founded what is now known around the world as Coerver® Coaching. Since then, the Coerver® Coaching curriculum has been expanded to encompass all technical aspects of the game.

Charlie Cooke, Wiel Coerver and Alfred Galustian

1 v 1 is only one part of the Coerver® Curriculum, butremains extremely important. The curriculum is constantly being updated and this book focuses on our latest approach to 1 v 1 teaching.

Section One

The Move Sets

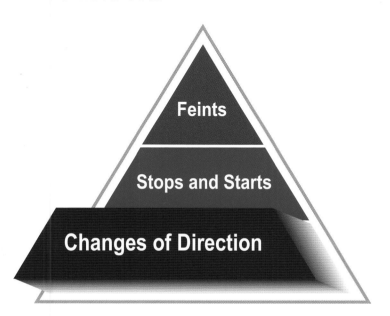

Move Set A
The Cut

A The Classic Cut

Feints

Stops and Starts

Changes of Direction

Where:

Across the goal.

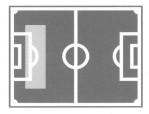

When:

Your opponent is in front of you.

Step 1

Push the ball forward.

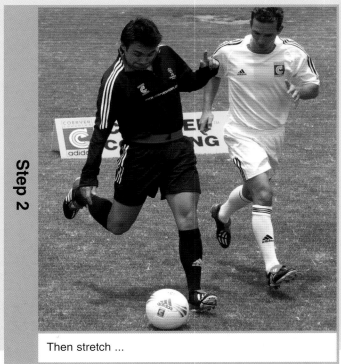

Step 2

Then stretch ...

Step 4

As you do this, turn with the ball.

Step 3

... and with the outside of your foot, stop the ball.

Step 5

Now you have shielded the ball, you can go in another direction.

Tips for players:

1 For the most effective outside cut, try to make sure the ball is well ahead of you.

2 Try to stay low and cut the ball with your ankle, rather than a stiff straight leg, so that you have a soft and flexible touch and can accelerate out of the move strongly.

3 As soon as you complete the move, look up to see where your opponents and teammates are.

A1 The Double Cut

Feints

Stops and Starts

Changes of Direction

Where:

Down the wing.

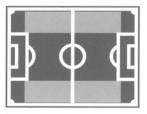

When:

Your opponent is beside you when shielding the ball.

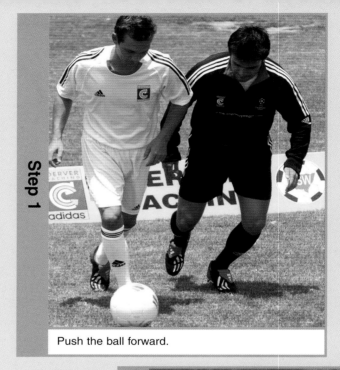

Step 1

Push the ball forward.

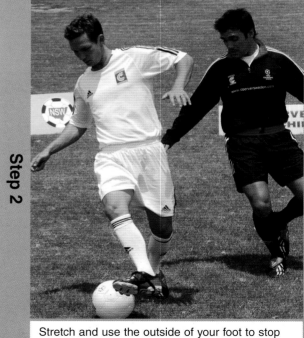

Step 2

Stretch and use the outside of your foot to stop the ball (outside cut).

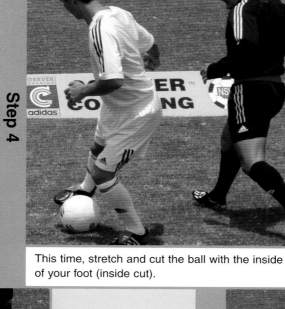

Step 4

This time, stretch and cut the ball with the inside of your foot (inside cut).

Step 3

Turn and push the ball backwards.

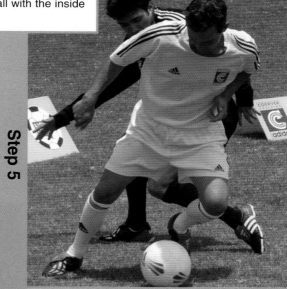

Step 5

Turn at the same time and continue in your original direction.

Tips for players:

1 Try to have the ball in front of you so you can reach and cut to save ground.

2 Turn quickly with only one touch.

3 Stay low to protect the ball, and so you can accelerate strongly out of the move.

A2 The Twist-off

Where:

In the middle of the field.

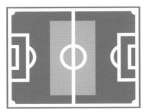

When:

Your opponent is in front of you.

Step 1

Fake a kick ...

Step 2

... but instead, control the ball with the outside of the kicking foot.

Step 4

With the outside of your pivot foot, push the ball to the side of your opponent.

Step 3

Pivot on the step-around foot and turn at the same time.

Step 5

Accelerate past your opponent.

Tips for players:

1 You need to be at an angle as you face an opponent for the twist-off move to work.

2 Try to bend your knee slightly and stay low as you cut the ball, so you can spin smoothly and accelerate quickly from a low centre of gravity.

Skill Drill A

- Feints
- Stops and Starts
- Changes of Direction

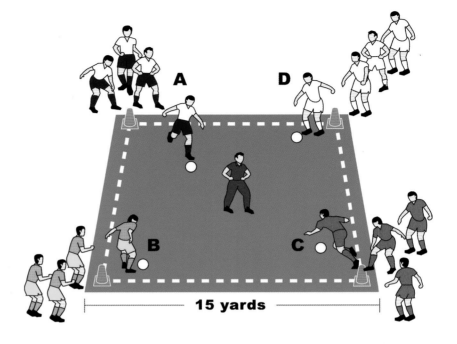

15 yards

Practice time:

Ten to 12 minutes.

Set-up:

- A grid of 15 x 15 yards.
- Four groups of up to five players on each corner of the square.
- First player in each group starts with the ball.

Action for single or double cut:

The first players in each group push the ball out and make the single or double cut. They then pass the ball to the next player in the group and sprint to the group to await their next turn.

Action for twist-off:

Players with the ball do toe taps (ie tapping the ball from foot to foot with the inside of each foot, while on the spot). On the coach's signal, one player dribbles towards the coach, makes the twist-off and passes to the next group. He then joins that group and awaits his next turn.

Variation:

The coach can act as a limited pressure defender by stepping in to challenge one of the players coming towards him. *Limited pressure* is where rather than trying to win the ball from the attacker, a teammate or coach helps by providing little or no pressure in the early learning period. The coach or teammate increases the pressure gradually as the move is learned and the player becomes more proficient.

Tip for coaches:

To do the cut moves correctly, remind players to have the ball well in front of them and to reach with their leg to save ground and cut with the minimum number of touches (whether cutting with the inside or outside of their foot).

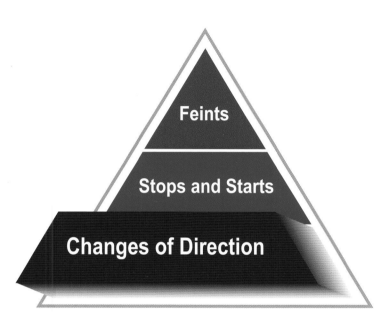

Move Set B
The Hook-turn

B The Hook-turn

Feints

Stops and Starts

Changes of Direction

Where:

Along the wings.

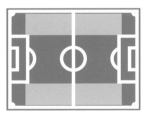

When:

Your opponent is running at your side.

Step 1

Push the ball forward.

Step 2

Fake a cross, but instead ...

Step 4

Turn ...

Step 3

... use the inside of your kicking foot to hook the ball behind your standing leg.

Step 5

... and take the ball in the opposite direction with your opposite foot.

Tips for players:

1 Make sure that the fake cross is realistic. You want your opponent to be off balance, trying to block it.

2 Try pulling the ball back with the toe part of your sole, to make the move lighter and quicker.

B1 The U-turn

Feints

Stops and Starts

Changes of Direction

Where:

Along the wing or in the middle of the field.

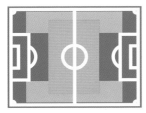

When:

Your opponent is in front of you.

Step 1

Fake a kick with your right foot, but ...

Step 2

... use the toe part of the sole of your kicking foot ...

Step 4

Then, with the inside of your opposite foot push the ball ...

Step 3

... to pull the ball to the other side of your opponent.

Step 5

... and accelerate away from your opponent.

Tips for players:

1 You should also practise this move using your left foot.

2 Use the front part of your sole to pull the ball around.

3 As you turn your body, make sure you shield the ball from your opponent.

B2 The U-turn Step-over

Feints

Stops and Starts

Changes of Direction

Where:

In the middle of the field.

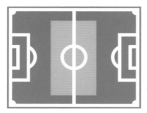

When:

Your opponent is to the side of you as you are running forward.

Step 1

Push the ball forward.

Step 2

Slow down and use your sole to pull the ball around, so you are shielding it from your opponent.

Step 4

... to the other side.

Step 3

Step over the ball with the same foot ...

Step 5

Turn, and with the outside of the same foot, accelerate in the direction you were going in originally.

Tips for players:

1 Use the bottom of your toes to stop and turn the ball.

2 Shielding is an important skill. Here, you are combining shielding the ball with creating space by sending your opponent the wrong way with a step-over feint.

Skill Drill B

Feints

Stops and Starts

Changes of Direction

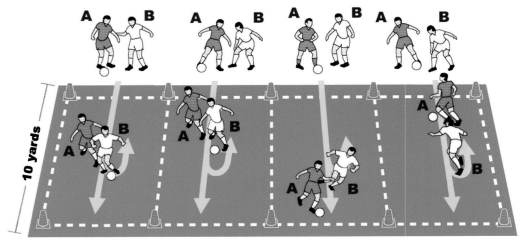

10 yards

Practice time:

Eight to ten minutes.

Set-up:

- An area of ten yards in length.
- Players in pairs.
- Player A has the ball. Player B is a limited pressure opponent (no tackling).

Action:

- One pair at a time, players race to either end line with the option of going back to the start line. The benefit of learning a change of direction move is that you have the option of going one way or the other, so it's difficult for your opponent to know where you're going.
- Player B, however, cannot start until A has touched the ball.
- A and B change roles after each contest. The first player back is the winner.

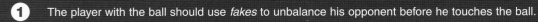

Tips for coaches:

1 The player with the ball should use *fakes* to unbalance his opponent before he touches the ball.

2 Remind players they are accelerating from a standing position, so the first few yards need to be run as quickly as possible.

Feints

Stops and Starts

Changes of Direction

Move Set C
The Step-on

C The Step-on

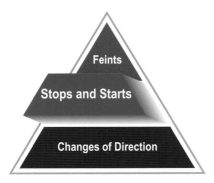

Where:

Along the wings.

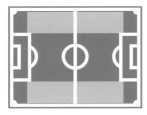

When:

Your opponent is to the side of you.

Step 1

As you run down the wing with your opponent chasing after you ...

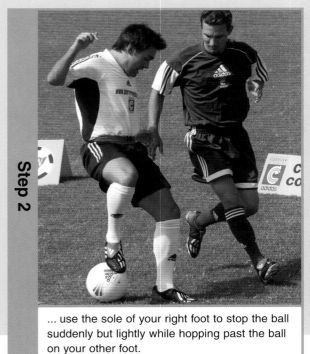

Step 2

... use the sole of your right foot to stop the ball suddenly but lightly while hopping past the ball on your other foot.

Step 4

Turn, and with the outside of your left foot ...

Step 3

When you land with both feet on the ground, the ball will be behind you.

Step 5

... go past your opponent.

Tips for players:

1   You should also practise this move using the opposite feet.

2   While hopping on one leg, step lightly with your sole on top of the ball to stop it.

3   Your momentum should take you past the ball with both feet landing beyond it. Now turn and take the ball.

C1 The Pull-push

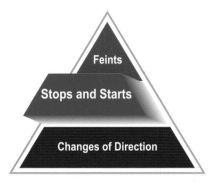

Feints

Stops and Starts

Changes of Direction

Where:

Along the wings.

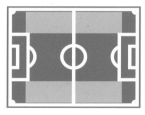

When:

Your opponent is to the side of you as you are running along the wing.

Step 1

As you run down the line ...

Step 2

... slow down a little and stop the ball with your sole.

Step 3

Drag the ball back a few inches.

Step 4

Then, push the ball forward again and accelerate away from your opponent.

Tips for players:

1. Stop the ball with the foot that's furthest away from the opponent.

2. This move is very difficult if you are running fast, so slow way down before you drag the ball back.

3. Use the inside of your foot to push the ball forward and, at the same time, stay low and lean forward for good acceleration.

4. Go into this move slowly, then accelerate out of it fast for an effective change of pace.

C2 The Step-kick

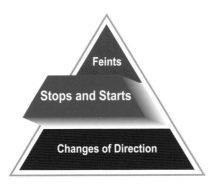

Feints

Stops and Starts

Changes of Direction

Where:

Across the goal or down the wings.

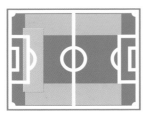

When:

Your opponent is to the side of you.

Step 1

As you run forward ...

Step 2

... slow down slightly and stop the ball with your sole.

28

Step 3

At the same time, use the toe of your opposite foot to kick the ball forward.

Step 4

Now you have created space, and can accelerate away from your opponent.

Tips for players:

1 Make sure your step-on foot is still touching the ball when your opposite foot kicks the ball forward.

2 Don't jump on the ball when you stop it, or you may hurt yourself. Step on the ball lightly.

3 Practise this move to develop a good touch so you don't over-kick the ball and lose control of it.

C3 The High Wave

Where:

Across the goal or down the wings.

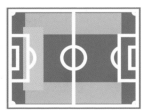

When:

Your opponent is to the side of you.

Step 1

As you run forward ...

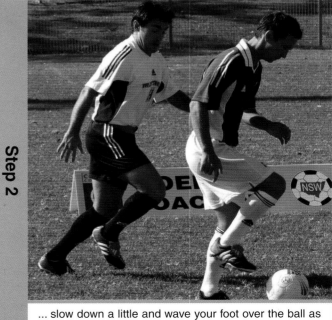

Step 2

... slow down a little and wave your foot over the ball as if you're going to stop it with your sole.

Step 3

Instead, bring your foot back behind the ball and ...

Step 4

... push it forward with the instep (laced part of shoe) and accelerate.

Tips for players:

1 Keep your foot as near to the ball as possible without touching it, to make it look like you're going to stop it or strike it.

2 Bend your knees slightly and lean over the ball a little so you can accelerate away quickly.

C4 The Half-pull Spin

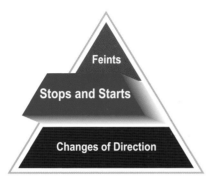

Where:

Near a corner.

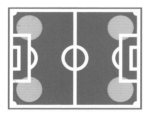

When:

Your opponent is behind you.

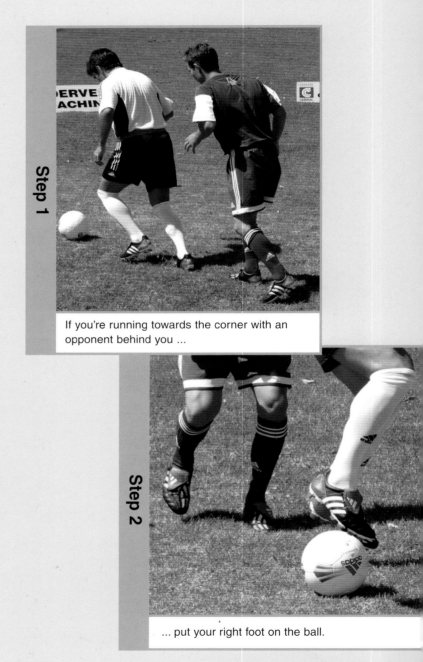

Step 1

If you're running towards the corner with an opponent behind you ...

Step 2

... put your right foot on the ball.

Step 4

... and drag the ball back with your left foot.

Step 3

At the same time, turn ...

Step 5

Now you are facing your opponent 1 v 1, use a feint to go past him.

Tips for players:

1   Use the tip of your sole on the top of the ball to stop it, and pivot around the ball at the same time.

2   As you face your opponent, drag the ball away from him and back towards you, stepping back for more space to take him on 1 v 1.

Skill Drill C

Feints

Stops and Starts

Changes of Direction

Practice time:

Ten to 12 minutes.

Set-up:

- Area of 25 x 20 yards
- Groups of four or five players, each with a ball.

Action:

- Player As go down one lane and to the back of Group B.
- Player Bs do the same down their lane and go to the back of Group A.
- Next player goes when teammate in front reaches the first cone.
- Players make any of the moves in the Step-on Set in the middle of the lane.

Variations:

Players can make two different moves; one at each cone.

Tip for coaches:

Players should slow down before making any of the moves in the Step-on Set but come out of each move quickly.

Move Set D
The Scissors

D The Scissors

Feints

Stops and Starts

Changes of Direction

Where:

In front of your opponent's goal.

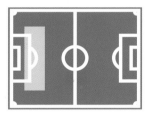

When:

Your opponent is in front of you.

Step 1

Step around the front of the ball ...

Step 2

... and lean in that direction.

Step 3

As your foot touches the ground, use the outside of your opposite foot to take the ball ...

Step 4

... in the opposite direction, and away from your opponent.

Tip for players:

Try to keep the ball near you, so you can step around close to the ball and low to the ground with good balance (ie on the ball of the foot, rather than the heel), and make a move.

D1 The Double Scissors

Feints

Stops and Starts

Changes of Direction

Where:

Down the wing.

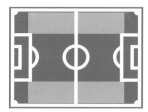

When:

Your opponent is in front of you.

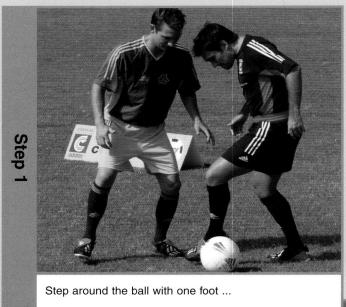

Step 1

Step around the ball with one foot ...

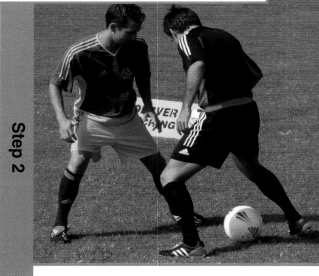

Step 2

... to the other side of it.

Step 4

... to the other side.

Step 3

Now do the same with your other foot, stepping around the ball ...

Step 5

Then, with the outside of your original step-around foot, take the ball past your opponent.

Tips for players:

1 This is a double move, so you will need a little extra space to make it. Don't try it if your opponent is very close or closing in fast.

2 Don't reach or lean back. Try and stay close to the ball so you're well balanced and can make a fast move.

39

D2 The Step-over Scissors

Feints

Stops and Starts

Changes of Direction

Where:

In front of goal.

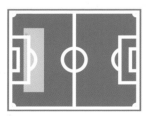

When:

Your opponent is in front of you.

Step 1

Fake a kick with your right foot ...

Step 2

... and step around the ball instead.

Step 4

... to the other side of the ball.

Step 3

Then step around it again with the same foot ...

Step 5

Now push the ball with the outside of your opposite foot and accelerate away.

Tip for players:

This is a double feint and each foot action must be quick so that the whole move happens fast, in order to prevent the opponent stepping in and stealing the ball.

Skill Drill D

Feints

Stops and Starts

Changes of Direction

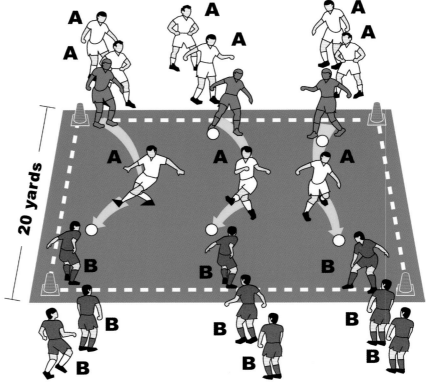

A A A A A

A

20 yards

A A A

B B B

B B B

B B B

Practice time:

Eight to ten minutes.

Set-up:

Players in groups of three or four, standing in lines about 20 yards apart with the front players of each group facing each other.

Action:

The first player of each group starts with the ball and goes into the middle, makes a move, passes to the opposite player and then sprints back to that group and awaits his next turn.

Variations:

1 Do two single moves, then pass.

2 Do three single moves, then pass.

3 Do four single moves, then pass. Increase the distance between groups to 30 yards.

Tips for coaches:

1 Tell players to slow down before making the move, especially if they're beginners.

2 When players pretend to go right but then go to their left, they should pass the ball with their left foot and vice versa.

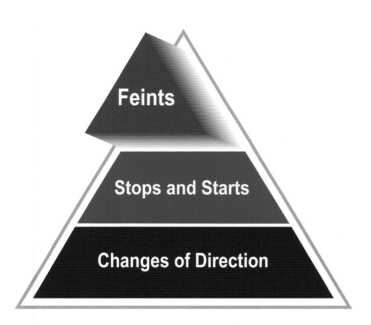

Move Set E
The Side-step

E The Single Side-step

Feints

Stops and Starts

Changes of Direction

Where:

In front of your opponent's goal.

When:

Your opponent is in front of you.

Step 1

Move your foot as if to take the ball to the side with the outside of your left foot.

Step 2

Instead, step beyond it and to the other side ...

Step 3

... and take the ball in the opposite direction with the outside of your right foot.

Step 4

Accelerate away from your opponent.

Tips for players:

1. You can start with either right or left foot. In this way, you can beat opponents either to the left or to the right.

2. Keep behind the ball as you step to the side of it.

3. Lean over to throw your opponent off balance.

45

E1 The Double Side-step

Where:

On the wing or in front of goal.

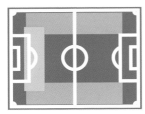

When:

Your opponent is in front of you.

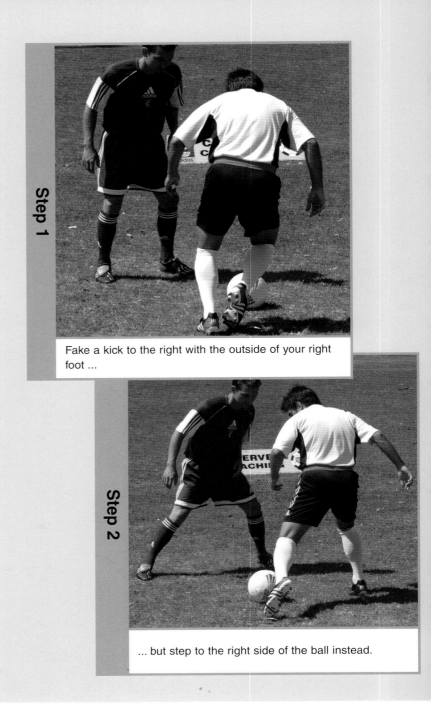

Step 1

Fake a kick to the right with the outside of your right foot ...

Step 2

... but step to the right side of the ball instead.

Step 3

Now fake a kick to the left with the outside of your left foot ...

Step 4

... but step to the left of the ball instead.

Step 5

With the outside of your right foot, take the ball to the right and accelerate away from your opponent.

Tips for players:

1 You should also practise this move using the opposite feet.

2 Make the side-steps short and fast; not long or slow.

3 Stay low so that when it's time to *go*, you get maximum acceleration.

4 For double moves you need a little more space, so look up and see how quickly the opponent is moving towards you before deciding if a double move is possible.

Skill Drill E

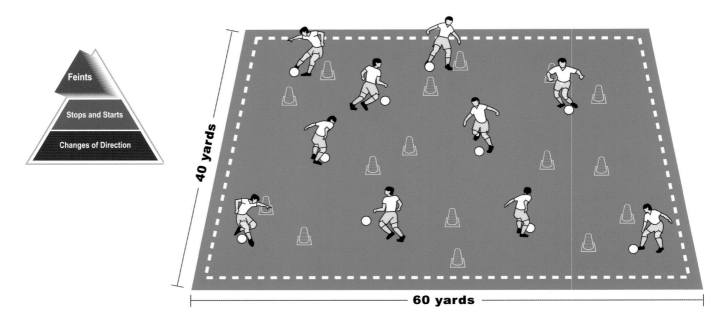

Feints

Stops and Starts

Changes of Direction

40 yards

60 yards

Practice time:

Five to eight minutes.

Set-up:

- Mark off an area of 40 x 60 yards.
- Up to 12 players, each with a ball.
- Eight three-yard-wide mini-goals.

Action:

On the coach's signal, players have to go through any of the eight mini-goals. As they go through each goal, they must make the move specified by the coach. Players then proceed to a different goal to make the move and *score* again. Allow 45 seconds to see how many *goals* players can score.

Variation:

You can also do this without the ball as a fitness exercise.

Tip for coaches:

Players must look up and be aware of what's going on around them. Otherwise, they will find themselves trying to go through the same goal as their teammates and colliding.

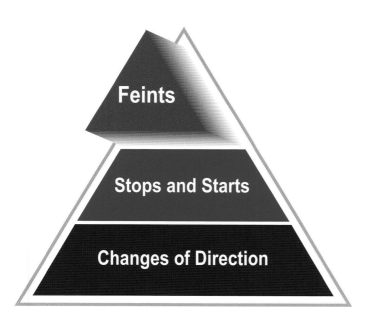

- Feints
- Stops and Starts
- Changes of Direction

Move Set F
The Step-over

F The Step-over

Where:

In front of goal.

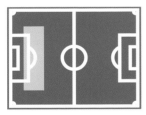

When:

Your opponent is in front of you.

Step 1

Approach the ball as if you're going to pass or strike it.

Step 2

Step over the ball instead, so your foot lands on the other side of it ...

Step 3

... and with the outside of the step-over foot, push the ball in the opposite direction.

Step 4

Accelerate past your opponent.

Tips for players:

1 Keep the ball close, and not far out in front of you.

2 Keep your step-around foot close to the ball, as if striking it low to the ground for a quick action.

3 When you step around the ball, turn your hips and upper body to trick your opponent into moving in that direction. This will also help you accelerate powerfully out of the move in the opposite direction; like a spring uncoiling.

F1 The Double Step-over

Feints

Stops and Starts

Changes of Direction

Where:

In front of goal.

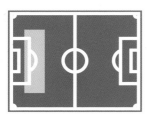

When:

Your opponent is in front of you.

Step 1

Fake a kick with your left foot.

Step 2

Instead, step around the ball.

Step 4

Instead, step around it again ...

Step 3

Then fake a kick with your right foot.

Step 5

... and use the outside of that foot to push the ball past your opponent and accelerate.

Tips for players:

1 Don't get too close to your opponent. For double moves (ie combinations of two separate moves), you need more space between you and your opponent. A gap of approximately 1.5 to 2 yards should allow you to complete the moves and prevent your opponent from stealing the ball.

2 Try to keep the ball close and under you as much as possible so you can step around fast while protecting it. This will also mean you're not reaching and leaning back to balance, and stepping around higher than necessary.

F2 The Pull Through Step-over

Feints

Stops and Starts

Changes of Direction

Where:

In front of goal.

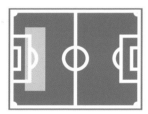

When:

Your opponent is in front of you.

Step 1

Stop the ball with your sole.

Step 2

Step around it with the same foot ...

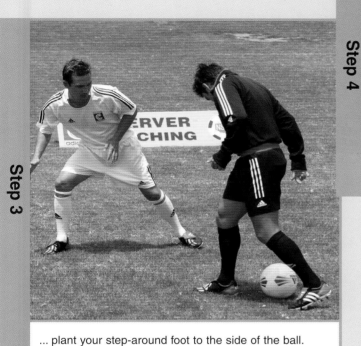

Step 3

... plant your step-around foot to the side of the ball.

Step 4

Pull the ball to the front with the instep of the trailing foot.

Step 5

With the outside of the original step-around foot, take the ball to the side of your opponent and accelerate away.

Tips for players:

1 Don't kick the ball with your trailing foot, but pull it forward with your instep as you step forward.

2 As the ball rolls forward, push it with the outside of the step-around foot and accelerate to the side.

F3 The Slap Step-over

Where:

Down the wings or with your back to the sideline.

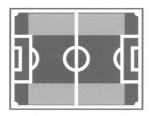

When:

Your opponent is in front of you.

Step 1

Use the sole of your foot to pull the ball sideways across your body.

Step 2

As the ball travels across, use the opposite foot to step around it ...

Step 3

... and to the other side of it.

Step 4

Now with the outside of the step-around foot, take the ball down the line.

Tips for players:

1   As soon as you pull the ball across, begin your step-over movement.

2   When you step around the ball, step as if you are going to strike the ball and turn your hips so the ball is shielded by your body.

Skill Drill F

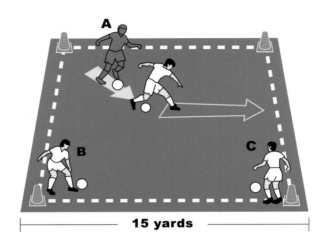

15 yards

Practice Time:

Eight to ten minutes.

Set-up:

- A square of 15 x 15 yards.
- Players A, B and C, each with a ball, start at a corner cone.

Action:

Players take turns, one after the other, making any of the step-over moves. They then accelerate to the nearest point of one of the lines on either side of the teammate facing them, and await their next turn.

Variation:

You can make this drill limited or full pressure by adding a player in the middle of the square who challenges for the ball. *Limited pressure* is where rather than trying to win the ball or hinder the player with the ball, a teammate or coach helps by providing little or no pressure in the early learning period. The teammate increases the pressure gradually as the move is learned and the player becomes more proficient. *Full pressure* is when the teammate applies 100% pressure and tries to win the ball.

Tip for coaches:

Tell players to look before and after they make their move so they can see which side to accelerate to.

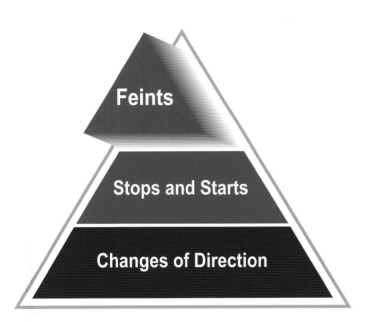

Feints

Stops and Starts

Changes of Direction

Move Set G
The Drag Push

G The Drag Push

Feints

Stops and Starts

Changes of Direction

Where:

Along the wings.

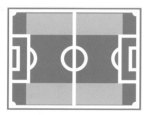

When:

Your opponent is in front of you.

Step 1

As you face your opponent, drag the ball across your body with the inside of your foot.

Step 2

Then, suddenly switch and use the outside of the same foot ...

Step 3

... to push the ball to the outside of your opponent.

Step 4

Accelerate down the wing.

Tips for players:

1 As you pull the ball across your body, lean to the side so your opponent thinks you are going in that direction.

2 As you drag the ball across your body, take a small hop on the standing leg. This enables you to change direction and accelerate away strongly.

G1 The Reverse Drag Push

Where:

Along the wings.

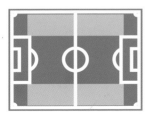

When:

Your opponent is in front of you.

Step 1

While facing your opponent ...

Step 2

... use your inside main foot to drag the ball across your body.

Step 4

As the stepping foot touches the ground, lean in the opposite direction and ...

Step 3

As the ball travels across your body in one direction, step in the opposite direction, as if to take the ball that way with the outside of the stepping foot.

Step 5

... push the ball with the outside of the other foot and accelerate past your opponent.

Tips for players:

1 It is important to be able to use both feet. Many of the moves like this one need two feet working together so you can operate on either wing, to cut inside, pass or shoot.

2 The side-step behind the ball should be short and fast.

G2 The Whip

Feints

Stops and Starts

Changes of Direction

Where:

In front of goal.

When:

Your opponent is in front of you.

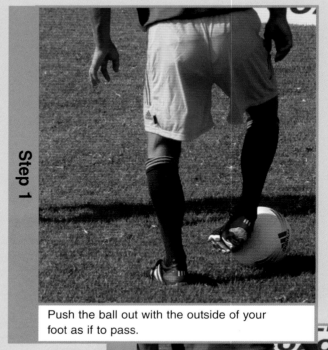

Step 1

Push the ball out with the outside of your foot as if to pass.

Step 2

As you push it out, switch your foot to the other side of the ball instead ...

Step 4

... flick the ball across your body.

Step 3

... and with the inside of your foot ...

Step 5

With the outside of your opposite foot, push the ball and dribble away from your opponent.

Tips for players:

1 Your foot should stay on the ball until you flick it back across you; it is one movement.

2 Push the ball as far out to the side as you can, to make your opponent move as much as possible in that direction.

G3 The Drag Scissors

Feints

Stops and Starts

Changes of Direction

Where:

Along the wings.

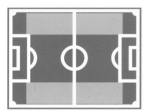

When:

Your opponent is in front of you.

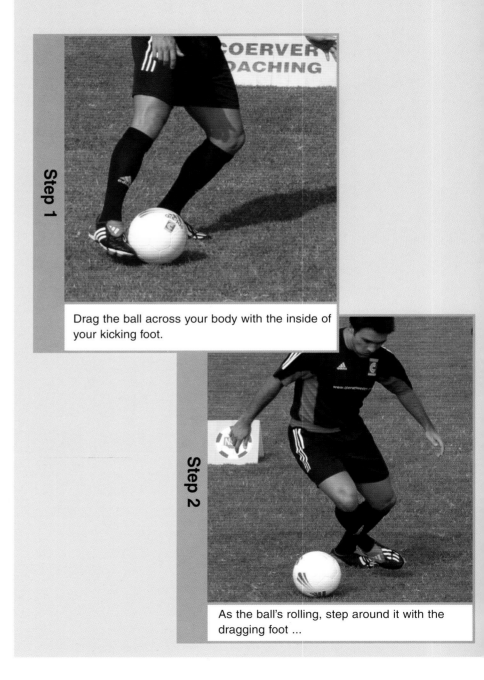

Step 1

Drag the ball across your body with the inside of your kicking foot.

Step 2

As the ball's rolling, step around it with the dragging foot ...

Step 4

Then take the ball with the outside of the other foot ...

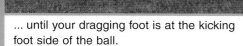

Step 3

... until your dragging foot is at the kicking foot side of the ball.

Step 5

... past your opponent and accelerate.

Tips for players:

1. This is a difficult move, so try it slowly at first.

2. The same foot that drags the ball steps around it.

3. Step strongly to the side to throw your opponent off balance.

Skill Drill G

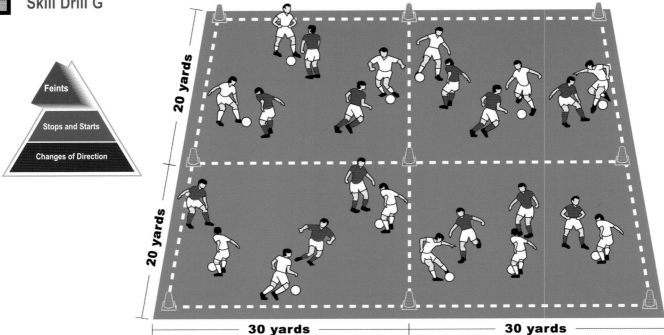

Practice time:

Eight to ten minutes.

Set-up:

- Four grids, each approximately 20 x 30 yards.
- Six players in each grid area.
- Three players with the ball are attackers; three others are limited pressure opponents.

Action:

Players dribble in the grid area. Players without the ball jog around the area. On the coach's signal, players with balls pass to players without balls and challenge as limited pressure opponents. The receiving players make moves and the sequence is repeated.

Tips for coaches:

1 Tell players to keep their heads up so they can judge the space they need in order to attack.

2 It is difficult to do any of the moves in The Drag Push Set, without slowing down or stopping the ball just before the move.

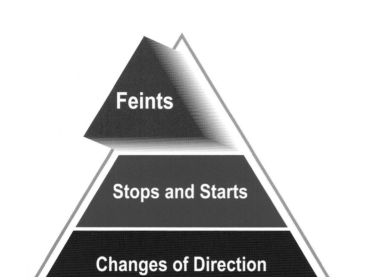

Move Set H
The Shimmy

H The Shimmy

Where:

With your back to the goal.

When:

Your back is to your opponent.

Step 1

Lift your heel and turn your knee inward as if to kick the ball ...

Step 2

... but stop just before you touch it.

Step 3

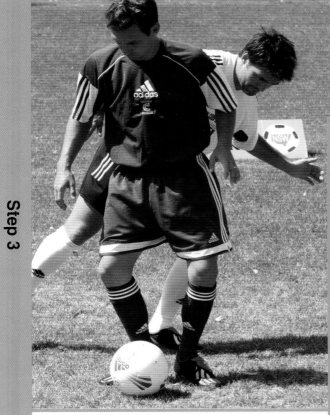

Turn ...

Step 4

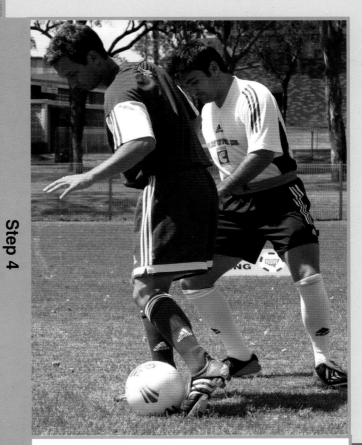

and spin past your opponent using your opposite foot.

Tip for players:

You will be more deceptive if you turn your hips towards the ball and drop the shoulder above the standing foot when you lift your other foot to fake the kick.

H1 The Hop

Where:

In front of goal.

When:

Your opponent is in front of you.

Step 1

Facing your opponent, lift the heel and turn the knee inwards as if to kick the ball ...

Step 2

... on the standing leg, but hop to one side of the ball.

Step 3

As your hopping foot touches the ground ...

Step 4

... use the outside of the opposite foot to accelerate past your opponent.

Tips for players:

1 Hop well to the side of the ball to make your opponent move out of position.

2 Lift the heel and turn the knee of your kicking foot inside to make the fake most effective.

Skill Drill H

Feints

Stops and Starts

Changes of Direction

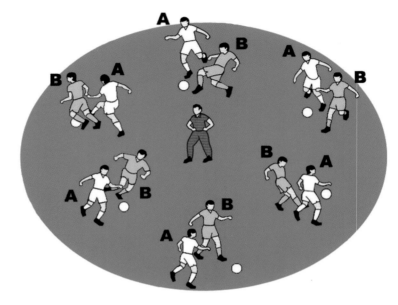

|— **15-yard radius** —|

Practice time:

Eight to ten minutes.

Set-up:

- Players in pairs.
- Give each pair one ball.

Action:

- Players jog in a circle.
- On the coach's signal, players make a move against their partners, who apply limited pressure.
- Players then pass the ball to their partners.
- Players jog again until the coach's signal, and then repeat the action the other way round.

Tip for coaches:

The limited pressure defender should give the player with the ball at least one yard of space.

Section Two

1 v 1 Skill Games

Introduction to Skill Games

We have selected some of our favourite skill games for use during training sessions.

As with the skill drills, each game can be used to reinforce 1 v 1 skills. However, whereas the skill drills were zero or limited pressure exercises (ie with no tackling by the opponent), the skill games are to be played at full pressure (ie with 100% tackling by the opponent).

Tips for coaches:

1 Don't expect much 1 v 1 success during these games until the players have begun to master the move techniques. It is important to conduct age- and ability-appropriate sessions. Don't try to do too much too soon.

2 Ideally players need to have as much full pressure practice as possible. However, the coach always has the option of mixing these with repetition exercises to improve the technique.

3 Bear in mind that every practice which teaches full pressure 1 v 1 attacking can also be used to teach 1 v 1 defending. The set-up, action and rules can all be the same. The only difference is that the coach should focus on the 1 v 1 defending aspects and give tips on these.

Skill Game 1

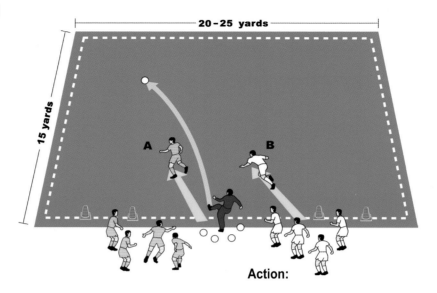

Practice time:

Ten to 15 minutes.

Set-up:

*   Two x two-yard-wide goals made with flags or cones placed 12 yards apart on the starting line.

*   Two teams on either side of the coach.

Action:

The coach passes the ball up-field and a player from each team sprints to get possession and score in either goal. Players must be within four yards of the goal line to shoot. If the defender wins the ball, he can score in either goal.

Variations:

You can progress from one, to two attackers versus two defenders.

Tips for coaches:

1 Coaches can play the ball to one side so that one of the players can get to the ball first, in order to keep the team competition even and lively.

2 When an attacker gets to the ball, he should try to hold his ground and not be forced away from the goals, even if he cannot turn immediately due to the opponent's pressure.

3 Instruct players to be as direct as possible and not give opponents time to recover. Remind them that scoring goals is the aim, and not using moves to show off.

4 Instruct players to try and turn to face opponents as early as possible, so as to put them on the defensive.

Skill Game 2

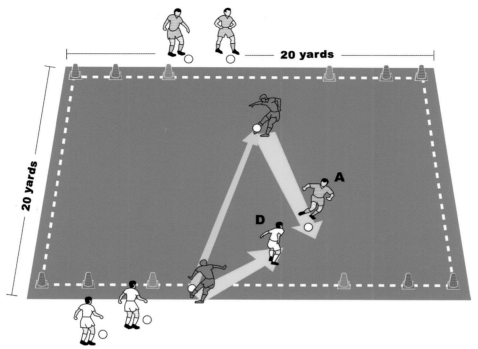

Practice time:

Eight to ten minutes.

Set-up:

- Twelve to 16 players.
- A 20 x 20 yard area.
- Two x one-yard-wide goals, one on each side.
- Larger goals between them on each end line.
- Defenders (D) with a ball, all on an end line.
- Attackers (A) facing the defenders on the opposite line.

Action:

- D1 passes to A1 and advances to defend the three goals on the defenders' end line. A1 tries to score by dribbling through any of the three goals. If the attacker scores in the middle goal, he wins three points and in the outside goals, one point.

- If the defender wins the ball, he can score by passing the ball through the attacker's goals. For the defender, scoring in the large goal wins one point and in the small goals, two points.

- Players change roles after each sequence. Change the opponents after the teams have played each other six times.

Variations:

From 1 v 1, you can progress to 2 v 2.

Tips for coaches:

1 Receivers should not wait for the ball, but should go and meet it.

2 The first touch of the receiver is crucial; ideally, it should not be too close to the body.

Skill Game 3

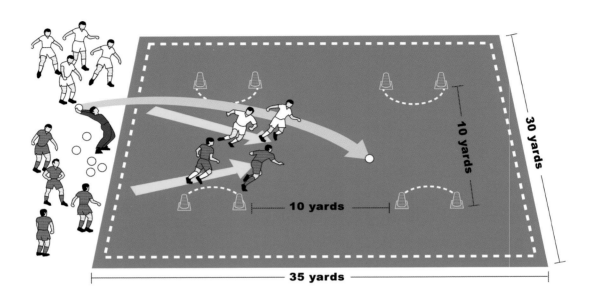

30 yards

10 yards

10 yards

35 yards

Practice time:

Ten to 12 minutes.

Set-up:

- A 30 x 35 yard field.
- Four small two/three-yard-wide goals facing outwards. (Players can only score into the goal from the outside.)

Action:

- Played 2 v 2.
- The coach plays the ball to the middle of the grid and two players from each team try to gain possession and score in any goals.
- The coach starts off another two pairs as soon as each goal is scored.

Variations:

You can play 3 v 3 or 4 v 4 in this set-up.

Tips for coaches:

1 Encourage players to use both feet to shoot.

2 Encourage players to use their teammates for fake passes and decoys. We start at 2 v 2, so that each player can practise his options – 1 v 1 or a pass.

3 Award two points for a one-touch score from a teammate's pass.

Skill Game 4

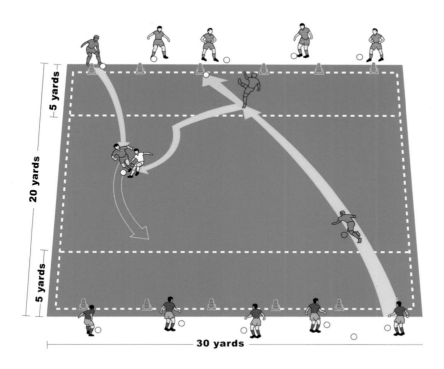

Practice time:

Ten to 12 minutes.

Set-up:

- A 20 x 30 yard field.
- Mark off a five-yard-wide shooting zone across the field in front of the goals, in which you place a row of six evenly spaced target cones.
- Ten players, each with a ball.
- The coach selects one player to start.

Action:

- The first player dribbles the ball to the opposite end and tries to knock down one of the cones with it. (No player can defend any of the cone targets.)
- As soon as the player shoots (he must be in the shooting zone), he immediately defends against one of the opposing players, who sets off toward the opposite target cones and tries to knock one of them down.
- This sequence of *attacker becoming defender* repeats until one team knocks down all the cones.

Variations:

You can play 2 v 2 in this set-up.

Tips for coaches:

1. Players can be numbered to avoid two players in the same team setting off at the same time.

2. Speed with the ball is essential for the attacker here, so don't touch the ball too many times.

Skill Game 5

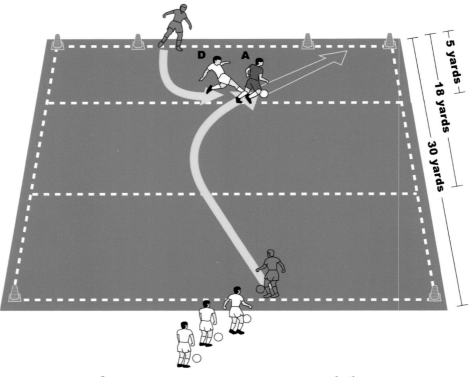

5 yards

18 yards

30 yards

Practice time:

Ten to 12 minutes.

Set-up:

- One player starts as a defender (D) on the middle of the end line.

- Attackers (A), each with a ball, line up 20 to 30 yards away.

- Mark the shooting line five yards from the goal.

Action:

- A1 starts with ball, and plays 1 v 1 against D.

- As soon as A1 shoots (he must be inside the shooting zone) or is tackled, he defends and A2 starts running with the ball towards goal and shoots (once inside the shooting zone). At the same time, the defender goes to the back of the attacker's line.

Variation:

From 1 v 1, you can progress to 2 v 2.

Tip for coaches:

Tell players to shoot with their left foot when they go to the left and with their right foot when they go to the right. If they change the shooting foot, they forfeit the yardage/space advantage they have gained from the initial move.

Skill Game 6

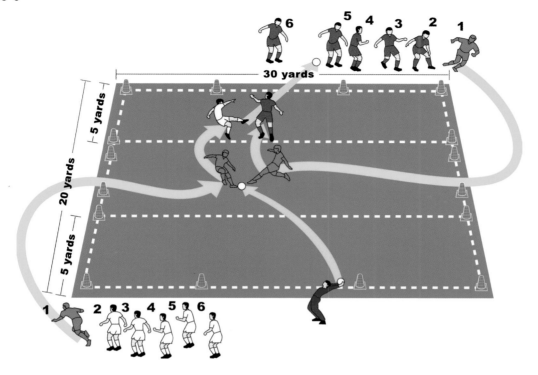

Practice time:

Ten to 12 minutes.

Set-up:

- A 20 x 30 yard field.
- The coach has a supply of balls.
- Mark a shooting line five yards from each goal.
- Cones at each corner of the field.
- Cone goals (*gates*) at either side of the halfway line.
- Line up two teams alongside each goal on the goal line.
- Number the players on each team.

Action:

The coach calls a number. The two opposing players with that number sprint through their respective gates and try to score (from inside the shooting line).

Variation:

- You can play 2 v 2, 3 v 3 or 4 v 4 using the same set-up.
- Increase or decrease the shooting zone to suit the level of the players. Use a larger zone for less skilled players.

Tip for coaches:

It's often the quickest player who wins the game, so tell players to be alert and ready for the call.

81

Skill Game 7

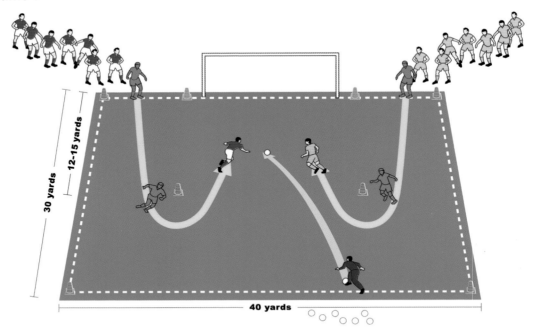

Practice time:

Ten to 12 minutes.

Set-up:

- The penalty area of a football field.
- Place cones one yard from each post to create two small goals.

- Place two cones 12 to 15 yards from the goal.
- Two groups of up to eight players positioned ten yards to either side of the goal.
- The coach in the middle, facing the goal with a supply of balls.

Action:

- The coach starts each contest by playing the ball.
- One player from each team must sprint around his respective cones.
- The first player to the ball tries to dribble and penetrate the six-yard box to score in one of the small goals either side of the main goal. Goals can only be scored from inside the six yard box.
- If the opponent wins the ball, he becomes the attacker.
- Players switch groups after each contest.

Tips for coaches:

1 The coach serves the ball to one side, not to the middle.

2 Make it clear 1 v 1 is only necessary when opponents are in the way. Otherwise, tell players to use speed to beat opponents.

Skill Game 8

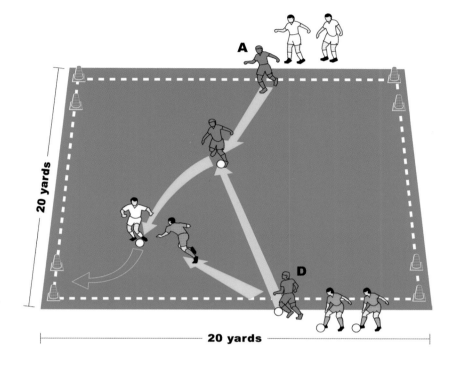

Practice time:

Ten to 12 minutes.

Set-up:

- Two groups, 20 yards apart.
- One group starts as attackers; the other as defenders.
- Each defender has a ball.
- Place two small one-yard-wide goals on either side.

Action:

- The defender passes to the attacker and challenges him.
- The attacker tries to dribble through any of the four mini goals.
- If the defender wins the ball, he tries to dribble it through any of the four goals.

Tips for coaches:

1. Tell players not to stop the ball, but to take it towards the target with their first touch.

2. When players have tried this a few times, begin to nominate moves for attackers to try, without telling the defenders the specified moves.

Skill Game 9

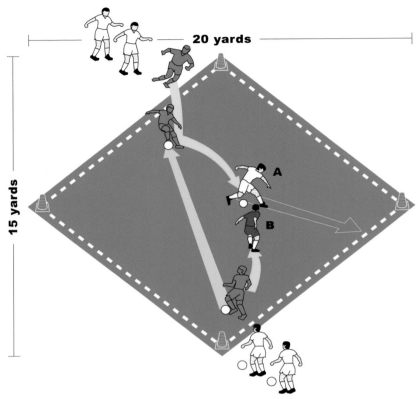

20 yards

15 yards

A

B

Practice time:

Twelve to 15 minutes.

Set-up:

• A 20 x 15 yard diamond shaped grid.

• Two groups (A and B) at either end of the grid.

• One group starts as defenders, each player with a ball.

Action:

• B passes to A and defends.

• A uses one of the moves to beat B and dribbles over the lines to B's right or left.

Tips for coaches:

1 Attackers should try using feints to create space in order to go past their opponent.

2 Once a player has created space, encourage the use of only one touch to get over either sideline. Explain that the more touches a player takes, the better the chance for the opponent to recover.

Skill Game 10

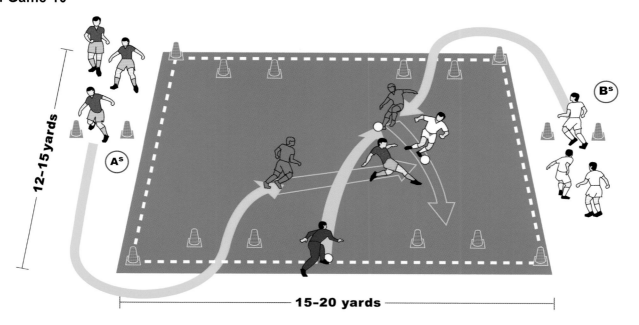

12–15 yards

Aˢ

Bˢ

15–20 yards

Practice time:

Twelve to 15 minutes.

Set-up:

- Four small goals on either side of the field.

- Two teams (A and B) at either end, lined up between two cones.

- The coach has a supply of balls.

Action:

- On the coach's signal, a player from each team sprints around a corner cone and through the first goal.

- The coach passes the ball to a B team player.

- B1 plays A1 1 v 1. B1 tries to dribble through either end goal; A1 tries to win the ball.

- The game is over if A1 gets the ball.

- Each team gets two tries to dribble through either end goal and score a point.

Tip for coaches:

Players shouldn't stop the ball when receiving it. They should try to take it first touch toward their target and, when blocked, use a move.

Section Three

General Advice for Coaches and Players

While the skills covered in this book are being taught and learnt, it is important for the coach and the player to bear in mind the following general advice.

Goals for Coaches

Plan ahead – Make sure the content of your practice is appropriate to the age and level of your players. Vary the sessions, as variation often keeps players focused. Be careful you don't try to do too much in one training session.

Make it fun – Make sure your session is fun, especially for young players. Keep a record of what works well for future use.

Communicate effectively – Be simple, clear and calm with your instructions. Don't shout. Smile, praise and encourage a lot.

Make it a truly team effort – Encourage your players to ask questions and think for themselves, and to be unafraid of making mistakes. This is how they will learn and grow. Listen to them and be patient.

Demonstrate the skills – Demonstrating is better than talking. If you are not comfortable with demonstrating skills, however, choose one of your better players to demonstrate. Be careful not to demonstrate too quickly, especially if the players are new to the skills. Always demonstrate what to do, rather than what not to do.

Goals for Players

Skill – You can never practise your skills too much. Soccer is a technical game and, as such, you need to constantly work on improving your individual skills. Remember though, that skills need to be used effectively in games to add to your team's performance and capabilities.

Speed – It is important to improve both your mental and physical speed in order to use your skills effectively in the game. Work on your mental speed, often called decision-making, by playing in small-sided games of 3 v 3 or 4 v 4. Build your physical speed by running with the ball – and remember that changing speeds when you are running with the ball can often deceive your opponents.

Stamina (fitness) – A good motto to follow is *respect your body*. Watch what you eat and drink, and keep as fit as you can by training (although be careful, and don't overdo it).

Sense – We use this word to mean *game understanding*. Here again, you need to play as much soccer as possible; especially small-sided games. Soccer is a wonderful game because each situation and moment in a game can be different, but the more you play the more you will be involved in the various problem-solving situations that occur in games.

Spirit – Here, the key words are always *do your best*. You can't win every game, so it's important that your attitude and resolve are always upbeat. Whether you are winning or losing, give your all.

Self-discipline – If you want to be a really good player you have to make time to practise often. This means sometimes you may have to give up social activities, for instance.

Self-confidence – This is most important. Sometimes it is the difference between being a very good player or not. You gain self-confidence by taking responsibility for your practice habits and experiencing improvement and success. To be successful you not only need good skills, but also a good attitude.

Sportsmanship – All players have an obligation to play the game fairly. Here, the key word is *respect*, for your teammates, your opponents, the referee and the game.

Smile – Even the best players in the world started playing soccer because they enjoyed it as youngsters, so the key words here are *enjoy the game*.

Section Four

Further Information

A large selection of Coerver® Coaching educational products and equipment is available. For more information or to purchase resources, visit the appropriate website below.

Resources

The following visual aids have been produced by Wiel Coerver, Alfred Galustian and Charlie Cooke.

On Video:

(1993) *Coerver Coaching Drill Series* (three-part series)

(1995) *The Creative Dribbler*

(1998) *A New Era* (three-part series)

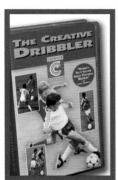

On DVD:

(2004) *Coerver Coaching Three-part Make Your Move Series*

Websites

Australia: www.coerveraustralia.com

China: www.coerver.com.cn

Europe: www.coervereurope.com

Japan: www.coerver.co.jp

Sweden: www.coerversweden.com

Thailand: www.coervercoachingthailand.com

UK: www.coerver.co.uk

USA: www.coerver-coaching.com

Section Five

Coerver Coaching Around the World

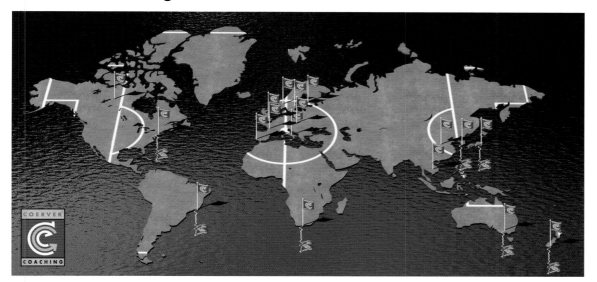

Coerver® Coaching has developed widely since the 1970s, and now has products, programmes and activities all over the world.

USA

Charlie Cooke (Director of the USA Programme) and Kristine Lilly (winner of two World Cups and Olympic Gold, and role model for all young players).

Coerver® Coaching has 35 licensees and operates in 40 states.

Of the 35,000 students who attend Coerver® Coaching events each year, over 30% are girls. Women's soccer is growing all over the world, and Coerver® hopes to contribute to this growth.

Brazil

Several Coerver® Coaching clinics for coaches and players have been organised over the past five years because skilful soccer is much admired in Brazil. This is a true test of the credibility of the Coerver® Coaching method.

Carlos Parriera, Head Coach, Brazilian World Cup Champions.

The reaction to Alfred (Galustian)'s courses in Brazil was excellent. Many former World Cup players and coaches attended, and it was obvious to us all that such a programme that encourages and teaches individual skills and creativity is needed by us, as much as by other countries.

Carlos Parriera

Japan

Coerver® Coaching Asian Director, Tom Byer.

Over 200 of young boys attending our Japan programmes have gone on to J-League Professional Club Youth Teams ... but we are equally proud of the many thousands who have improved and had a lot of fun.

Tom Byer

One of 42 nationwide Coerver® Coaching schools.

More than 10,000 young players a year go through the Coerver® Programme.

China

There are three schools in Shanghai, with 50 schools planned nationwide by 2008.

Sun Wen, FIFA World Player of the Year, teaching a young Coerver® student.

Korea

Coerver® Coaching trains coaches from the professional K-League in Korea.

Thailand

Many members of the Thailand FA attend annual Coerver® Coaching clinics.

Australia

Represented by the New South Wales Soccer Federation, Coerver® Coaching is regarded as one of Australia's top programmes. Many of the graduates from their elite programmes have gone on to represent the U17 National Team.

Coerver® student, Terry Antonis, winner of a nationwide competition to find the most skilful young player in Australia.

South Africa

Martin Clark, Coerver® Coaching Europe and South Africa Director.

09

Europe

Programmes and products in UK, France, Italy, Germany, Sweden and Norway.

Coaching clinics run at clubs such as Real Madrid (Spain), Bayern Munich (Germany), Olympique Marseille (France) and Arsenal (England).

Rene Meulensteen, who worked with Coerver for many years around the world. Rene is now Technical Coach at Manchester United, where Sir Alex Ferguson has been a long-time admirer of the Coerver® Coaching method.